Live Life be Strong With God

Be Stronger With God

Stephanie N. Howard

WESTBOW PRESS®
A DIVISION OF THOMAS NELSON
& ZONDERVAN

Copyright © 2015 Stephanie N. Howard.

All rights reserved. No part of this book may be used or reproduced by any means, graphic, electronic, or mechanical, including photocopying, recording, taping or by any information storage retrieval system without the written permission of the author except in the case of brief quotations embodied in critical articles and reviews.

This book is a work of non-fiction. Unless otherwise noted, the author and the publisher make no explicit guarantees as to the accuracy of the information contained in this book and in some cases, names of people and places have been altered to protect their privacy.
Scripture verses, unless otherwise noted, are taken from the King James Version (KJV) of the Bible.

Scripture quotations designated (ESV) are taken from *The Holy Bible, English Standard Version*. Copyright © 2000, 2001 by Crossway Bibles, a division of Good News Publishers. Used by permission. All rights reserved.

Scripture quotations designated (NASB) are taken from the *New American Standard Bible*. Copyright © 1960, 1962, 1963, 1968, 1971, 1972, 1973, 1975, 1977 by the Lockman Foundation. Used by permission.

Scripture quotations marked "NKJV" are taken from the *New King James Version*® (NKJV®), copyright © 1982 by Thomas Nelson, Inc. Used by permission. All rights reserved.

Scripture verses marked "NIV" are taken from the *Holy Bible, New International Version*®, *NIV*®. Copyright © 1973, 1978, 1984, 2011 by International Bible Society. Used by permission of Zondervan. All rights reserved.

WestBow Press books may be ordered through booksellers or by contacting:

WestBow Press
A Division of Thomas Nelson & Zondervan
1663 Liberty Drive
Bloomington, IN 47403
www.westbowpress.com
1 (866) 928-1240

Because of the dynamic nature of the Internet, any web addresses or links contained in this book may have changed since publication and may no longer be valid. The views expressed in this work are solely those of the author and do not necessarily reflect the views of the publisher, and the publisher hereby disclaims any responsibility for them.

Any people depicted in stock imagery provided by Thinkstock are models, and such images are being used for illustrative purposes only.
Certain stock imagery © Thinkstock.

ISBN: 978-1-5127-1185-1 (sc)
ISBN: 978-1-5127-1186-8 (hc)
ISBN: 978-1-5127-1184-4 (e)
Library of Congress Control Number: 2015914582

Print information available on the last page.

WestBow Press rev. date: 09/03/2015

Contents

Introduction vii
Chapter 1   Mr. and Mrs. Howard 1
Chapter 2   Flowers and Heavy Labor 5
Chapter 3   Many Blessings 9
Chapter 4   Growing Grace 13
Chapter 5   Sharing the News 25
Chapter 6   Feeling God's Direction 29
Chapter 7   Cut, Cut, Cut! 33
Chapter 8   If You Ask, He Will Call Upon You 37
Chapter 9   Wait and See 45
Chapter 10 My Second Time in the Hospital 59
Chapter 11 Home Sweet Home 67
Chapter 12 Praying for Friendship 71
Chapter 13 Pride and Depression Don't
            Mix with God's Plan 75
Chapter 14 Facing Reality 83
Chapter 15 God Makes Me Stronger 87

Introduction

I am Stephanie Howard, a Jesus freak. I love my Lord and Savior, and I love all he has done for me and for the ones I love dearly. I'm the mom of three extraordinary girls: Hunter, Jaelie, and Violett. I'm the wife of one of the kindest hearted men I know. His name is Josh.

I'm not a 1950s-style wife and mother, but I do try to take care of my family. The only time I have an apron on is when I'm cooking and baking. I host the holidays for both my and Josh's extended families. I put the needs of Josh and our girls before my own with a smile and delight. Driving the girls to their appointments and practices, ironing, and cleaning the house—I do all this as if there were nothing else in the world I would rather be doing. You can decide later if all of the claims I make here are true or not.

I'm the type of woman who doesn't wear makeup or fancy clothes every day. And on the occasions when I do, I feel like I'm playing dress-up. I love to wear my hair up, for playing with the girls or getting my hands dirty with housekeeping or landscaping. There's a show on TV my girls talk about that's called *What Not to Wear*.

People on that show say, "You need to look like you're celebrating every day like it's an event." I have a bit of a problem with that, as I do not always look fabulous. I've learned with help from my three girls how I should put myself together in the morning. They keep me in the loop. No one should have to walk around with a mom who is a hot mess. That's embarrassing, right? If it were up to me a smile would be the magic of my outfit, not makeup, hairdos, or accessories.

In my free time, I like to remodel our home, take pictures, do arts and crafts, watch movies, and plan events/occasions for family and friends. I love to be around people and to entertain them. I also like to be outdoors for long walks or runs.

As I have already said, I have three beautiful girls. Hunter is the oldest; Jaelie is the middle; and Violett is the youngest. I wouldn't be the same person today without them. They're all different and special in their own way.

Hunter is a beautiful young teenager. She loves singing and writing songs, drawing abstract pictures, being with friends, having sleepovers, playing softball, and baking treats. Her specialty is coffee cake. She also loves reading mystery books. She has a big heart for helping people and animals in need. One year, Hunter and her friends had a fund-raiser to help the local animal shelter. They were able to buy gift cards, dog and cat food, cat litter, and cat toys. If it were up to

Hunter, we would have a dozen animals at our house. She's very successful in school. Her favorite subject is Honors English, and she writes creative short stories. I believe that she has the potential to be a successful author in years to come.

Jaelie is a cute young girl. She loves to be with people, young or old. She is outgoing and full of life, always wanting to be going out or doing something fun and exciting. Jaelie uses her marvelous imagination when creating stories during her free playtime. She gives her all when doing schoolwork or playing softball. One of my most favorite things about Jaelie is that she's not afraid of trying new things. She's open-minded, and she's outspoken about what she's thinking.

Violett is an adorable little girl. She's hardworking and has determination when she puts her mind to something. The world is her stage, and she's always performing. She loves drawing, playing with Barbies and baby dolls, and participating in gymnastics and softball. Violett has plans to get a scholarship for being a left-handed pitcher and hitter so she can go to school to learn to be an actress or a supermodel. She practices with my dress clothes and high heels. Don't get me started on makeup—it is a must-have in Violett's world. She has big dreams. She looks up to her older sisters and acts like them sometimes.

It was about a year before Violett would be going to school all day when family and friends started to ask me a curious question: "What are your plans for a job?" If you would have asked me that question twelve years ago, I would have told you that I wanted to pursue early education, hairdressing, photography, or maybe even event planning. But at that time I was uncertain what I should or could do after spending a lot of time out of the workplace.

After I prayed for months, God picked me to become an inspirational author. I was just as surprised as anyone. I wasn't the most successful student in school because I have learning disability called dyslexia. It has always stood in the way of my confidence. I wouldn't allow myself to explore my creative side for fear of negative comments or even of embarrassing myself. I didn't want family and friends to see what I wasn't capable of.

That's the brilliant thing about God, though: he'll help people with their path and direction if they just simply ask him. His plan was for me to inspire others about what he can do, not only for me, but also for you. You just need to believe in him and in the words he puts before you, his Holy Word, the Bible. God has brilliant ideas. All is possible with him.

During my story, we will see how the Lord is still performing miracles. You will hear about my life before, during, and after the miracle he performed for me. I think that after you read my story, you will know that miracles are still possible today.

A friend once told me that in order to have a rainbow, you need rain. It warms my heart to know that tears bring joy in the end. And that's exactly what this book can do; bring out all kinds of emotions and thoughts; help you stop and smell the roses; let you feel the Holy Spirit guiding you and opening your heart and mind; and help you realize what is possible with God, not you, leading you on your path.

> *Life is like a book. Some chapters are happy/exciting, and other chapters can be disappointing/sad. But you don't know what happens next until you turn the pages.*

> *Thou therefore, my son, be strong in the grace that is in Christ Jesus. And the things that thou hast heard of me among many witnesses, the same commit thou to faithful men, who shall be able to teach others also.*
> —2 Timothy 2:1–2

The above verse opened my heart to the grace that Christ Jesus has for me and for you. He wants me to share my commitment to faith with men and women around me. I shall be successful in teaching others about our Lord and Savior. God is with us always and forever.

Chapter 1

Mr. and Mrs. Howard

> Therefore humble yourselves under the mighty hand of God, that He may exalt you in due time, casting all your care upon Him, for He cares for you.
> —1 Peter 5:6–7 (NKJV)

Before I tell you about my fantastic, supportive husband, Joshie, I would like to share with you how he and I came to be Mr. and Mrs. Joshua Howard. I was eighteen years old when I was, lying in bed thinking and praying about the relationship of three years I had just gotten out of with a remarkable, handsome, and smart guy who played a big role in my life by helping me find who I was, who I wanted to be, and what I wanted my husband to be. I've thanked God for that guide every day. Dave guided me in the right direction of having goals, purpose, and choices, encouraging me not to settle for anyone whom, or anything that, I didn't want for myself or my future.

Having that in mind, I prayed about my choice in the man I wanted God to send me. I told God I wanted a man who loved the Lord, was involved in his church, had family values, was hardworking, had goals of his own, and wanted, like I did, to travel and see this amazing world that God created, And this man should be one who did not drink or smoke.

Wow, what an amazing God we serve! Two weeks after I prayed that prayer, God sent me the most incredible man to later become my husband, Joshua Earl Howard. Joshua and I met at the drive-through window at McDonald's. I first knew Joshua as Mr. Root Beer because he was the only person I knew who ordered a large root beer with a ham, egg, and cheese bagel meal at five in the morning. Most people drink coffee, tea, water, or milk with their breakfast, not root beer! I would say to my coworkers and friends in the restaurant, "Mr. Root Beer is here," and they would know what to make.

On Valentine's Day morning, I was telling all of my customers "Happy Valentine's Day" with a joyful attitude. Then it was Josh's turn to pull up in his truck at 5:00 a.m. That's when he caught my eye. For the first time, I took the time to look at Mr. Root Beer's face. He was handsome and charming. He made me smile and feel tickly in my tummy right away. After I regained my composure, Josh returned the kind words back, "Happy Valentine's."

Mr. Root Beer was now at my drive-through window asking for my phone number. *What is he thinking? Stranger-danger warning!* The girl in me was, truthfully, very flattered, but I kindly said back to him, "No, thank you." Joshua had determination; he wasn't going to give up easily. He tried for several weeks. I finally asked for my mom's permission to give Joshua my phone number. Mama Susie said yes. I went to work the next day, and there was Mr. Root Beer in the drive-through asking me for my phone number once again. And, yes, I gave him my number.

That night, Joshua called me for the first time. We talked for a couple of hours. I thought to myself, *Joshua has every quality that I prayed for and more. I'm going to marry this guy someday.* When our call was over, I, jumping up and down with excitement, came out of my room and said to my mom and brother Doug, "I'm going to marry this guy."

Doug and my mom shook their heads. My mom said, "Stephanie, you're crazy. You just talked to him on the phone. How much could you possibly know about him in one phone call?"

And I said, "I know it, Mom. We're going to be together forever. Oh, and by the way, Mom, Joshua is on his way over right now to take me to dinner, as long as you are okay with that." (At eighteen years old, you should still ask your mom's permission to date, especially when the man you're going out with is five years older than you.) Mama Susie said that it was okay with her.

Josh's and my first date was at Applebee's. While sitting there, I listened to Joshua's stories and interests. What he said confirmed what I knew from our phone call earlier. I was definitely going to spend the rest of my life with Josh. That's how I became Mrs. Root Beer. Romantic, huh?

Chapter 2

Flowers and Heavy Labor

I love flowers—big or small, it doesn't matter. It's amazing how God has created such extraordinary, beautiful, and exotic flowers for all the seasons. When flowers and plants start popping up all over my yard, I go nuts with excitement. Every spring, I add more flowers and plants to the landscaping around the beautiful home that God has provided my family with.

During the middle of March 2010, Josh and I took on our largest landscaping project: we started putting boulders and river rocks along our large ditch, and we transplanted flowers, putting them in new areas around the yard. But I couldn't stop there. I needed to buy and add more flowers to finish off my fabulous design plan. I think I'm quite the landscaper.

After a couple of long days, I started to think and feel that this spring landscaping project was making me fatigued, dizzy, and weak. I was also having blurred vision, headaches, and a loss of appetite. I just wasn't myself. I could normally keep up with Josh and work right by his side—but not for this project. I needed to stop a lot to take minibreaks. I had to sit down and drink a lot of water. I had to make myself eat some fruit, too, just hoping I would regain my strength quickly so I could do my share.

Joshua is an unusual guy who thinks it's okay and normal to start work at 5:00 a.m. and not stop work until 5:00 p.m. Little does he know that's *not* normal. He's just a guy who was *very* blessed by God with not needing his beauty sleep. His phrase to all of us girls in the house is, "Get up and out of bed! You can sleep when you are dead." He's a wacko bird, right?

After a couple more weeks of getting the house and yard ready for outdoor games, cookouts and, birthday parties I continued to feel under the weather. I faced a new difficulty every other day. Also, I couldn't stay up for more than a couple of hours before I needed to rest. This was because I was nauseated. My headaches were turning into migraines, and I had trouble with weakness and numbness in my legs. When I would pick up Violett, I would quickly have to put her down because my legs would just give out on me. Thankfully, I never dropped her.

My mom and sister-in-law Kendra would call just to have some girl talk, and I would mention the trouble I was having. They were both very sweet, but each time we talked, they would tell me that I was too busy and that I needed to take a break and relax. I would reply, "I know you're right, but how do I stop? I love having my house and yard clean, being active with Josh and the girls, and keeping myself involved in the girls' schoolwork and PTO planning."

How many of us have the problem of being too busy?

The Lord has blessed my and Joshua's children with a love and talent for softball and with always wanting to be on the go with activities. When June came around, softball games and practices started. We were going nonstop. As the weeks passed, it became more difficult for me to keep up with the pace. Now I was starting to vomit in the morning while brushing my teeth. In addition, I was, becoming weaker and weaker every day. I couldn't stand the taste of certain foods or the odor of certain fragrances. I was struggling physically and emotionally because I wanted to be at every softball game and practice, every fellowship with family, and every get-together (having dinners, watching movies, and playing games). I didn't want to miss out on all the fun. Unfortunately, my body was telling me to sleep because I was too weak to do anything else.

It was July 2010 when I decided I couldn't make any more of my own diagnoses for my symptoms. It was time I got down to the bottom of what I was experiencing on a daily basis. I was trying very hard to feel better, but nothing I did was helping. I tried eating, drinking, and taking my vitamins differently. I tried changing my routine with Josh and the girls. I, a neat freak, even changed the way I kept up with the house.

I was having difficulty with all of the changes my body was going through. Not being able to resolve my health problems on my own was frustrating. It was time for me to call the doctors and find out why I was having all these symptoms. I made appointments with my family and eye doctors, and then I made an appointment with my gynecologist. I was having everything checked out. I didn't have time for this nonsense. I had better things to do and to think about than being worried about feeling bad all day long.

Deep down in my heart, I already knew that God had given me a great sense of humor about my declining health. During the months leading up to this point, when Josh would ask me why I was having so many bad headaches or other problems, I would reply by saying, "Mama has a brain tumor."

My first appointment was with my family doctor. He started by asking me many questions about how I was feeling overall and how I was responding to certain foods, the weather, and exercise. After checking out my ears, nose, and throat, he said I had a bad sinus infection, but he thought that wasn't all that was wrong with me. He also said he wanted to get some blood tests done, but first he wanted me to take some medicine for a few weeks to help clear up the sinus infection. So I went home and did what the doctor told me to do. I like to be a rule follower, not a rule breaker.

Chapter 3

Many Blessings

One of the greatest blessings that my family has is Joshua's particular job. We are truly blessed to work for a premiere Christian construction company called Kleckner Interior Systems (KIS). Larry and Mavis Kleckner have always had loving, warm hearts. Their many nice, wonderful gestures have benefited our family. During the summer of 2010 when I was unwell, they gave us a week's stay at a condo in Orlando, Florida. We were all amazed and grateful. If only everyone could be as blessed by marvelous people in their lives; how much better this world would be from day to day!

The whole family was very excited about going to Florida. We kept thinking about a pool, hot weather, no work, rest, relaxation, no schedule, and, yes, Disney World. Joshua and I had three beautiful, outstanding little girls who wouldn't go to Orlando without attending the Disney princess luncheon.

When we arrived in Orlando, we could feel the Florida warmth right away. The sun was beaming down, and its reflection in Josh's sunglasses was blinding. One thing I must say is that when Joshua has a golden tan, his smile steals my heart. He knows this about me, so he was excited to get a suntan going.

At the condo, we dropped our bags, put on our swimsuits, and headed to the first of six pool areas that were available to us.

The girls played on the waterslides while Joshua and I reflected on how big the girls were getting, what their accomplishments were, and in what directions they were going. We discussed our goals for them and our goals for ourselves as parents. Unfortunately for me, I had to cut my poolside time short because I was exhausted. I had to go back to the condo, find my soft pillow and cozy bed, and go to sleep until Joshua and the girls became waterlogged or sunburnt.

On our vacation, the girls always woke me by playing "hotel customer service desk." They took turns sitting at the desk in the room and acting like they were hotel clerks. Pretending that the phone was ringing, they answered by saying, "Concierge, Please hold." For such little girls, they sure knew how to act like high-class Fancy Nancies.

Having three princesses who loved horses, Joshua and I found a live performance called *"Arabian Nights"* at a dinner theater. We were able to see real horses ridden by knights and an Arabian princess being rescued by her royal Arabian knight. We all enjoyed eating out of wooden bowls and using only our hands instead of utensils. After the show, we decided to take our family photo with the horses and the cast of the performance. The girls were able to sit atop the horses for individual pictures. Memories were made that day, for sure.

What's a family trip without seeing family? While in Orlando, we went to visit Joshua's cousin Kenny, Kenny's beautiful wife, Brenda, and their kids. Brenda was kind to show me, and to tell me how much she loved her life with, her beautiful flowers and lemon trees. She knew a great deal about all the precious landscaping plants in her yard. The girls loved swimming in Kenny and Brenda's pool with no one else in it but them. Kenny and Brenda made us a remarkable home-cooked meal. The stories they told at the dinner table about the good old days with Grandpa and Grandma Howard were joyful to hear. As we were getting ready to go back to the condo, Brenda gave the girls all kinds of treasures. They loved being spoiled by her, and Brenda loved spoiling them just the same.

During our family's last night in the condo, Joshua and I sat around the table and talked about how wonderful this vacation was for us. We had the opportunity to regroup as husband and wife, as father and mother, and, most important, as God-serving people.

Chapter 4

Growing Grace

Now that we were home from vacation, it was time to get out the planners and my appointment books. School would be starting in a couple of weeks. Grr. This mama loves spending time with her girls, not sending them to school. The first appointment I needed to set up was for my blood work, but first I had an eye doctor appointment. I wanted to get that out of the way.

But before all that, I prayed that our Lord and Savior would use me as a servant to reach lost souls. I felt, after reading my Bible and growing stronger every day for the Lord, that it would be an honor if God picked me for one of his miracles.

It was Friday, August 13—scary, right? I was sitting in a chair in Dr. Carlson's office and praying to God, asking, "God, are you sure I need to tell the doctor about all the symptoms I've been having? Or is it something that I already have taken care of with my family doctor?"

I felt God tell me, "Yes, tell him. Dr. Carlson needs to know so he can help you."

I began by telling Dr. Carlson about my going to see my family doctor, who discovered that I had a sinus infection. I then mentioned that the family doctor wanted me to get blood tests done after my medicine was finished. I went on to tell Dr. Carlson about the blurriness, dizziness, headaches, weakness, and fatigue I'd been experiencing. He soon began my exam. At first it was like all the other exams, but it quickly changed. Dr. Carlson asked more questions about my symptoms. After I answered him, he said he needed to step out of the room and talk with another doctor. I was thinking I had an infection in my eyes.

After a bit, Dr. Carlson and Dr. Buck both came into the room and said they wanted to run some more tests in the office that day. One of them said that I needed to make an appointment for an MRI as soon as possible! After I finished my tests in the office, Dr. Carlson, while walking me to the checkout, thanked me for staying longer. He then said, one more time, "Schedule the MRI as soon as you get home."

I smiled happily and said, "Okay, Dr. Carlson."

The first thing I did when I got home was what the doctor had told me to do. I made my MRI appointment and then scheduled my blood work for nine the following Monday morning. I wanted Joshua to know what happened at the eye doctor appointment. He sounded worried, but he seemed happy that I was finding out why I was having all the headaches and other symptoms. Again, I joked with him and said it was because "Mama has a brain tumor."

That weekend, our family celebrated my youngest daughter's, Violett's, fourth birthday. We had homemade sloppy jay-jays (this is what we like to call sloppy joes at our house), chips, Maw's potato salad, and Mimi's veggie pizza. And what's a party without delicious, giant cupcakes with big, yummy cherries on top? The precious thing about birthday parties is that you're creating memories that you might need at a key time in your life when you are needing to find happiness, joy, or love.

On Monday morning, a caring face at the check-in desk welcomed me once I arrived at the surgical center. The woman directed me to the nurse's station where I would be having my blood work done. You would think that after having three kids I would be fine with getting my blood drawn, but such is not the case! Needles and blood are not my favorite things to see. The nurse did a remarkable job, though. I didn't see or feel a thing. Praise the Lord! After she was done, she sent me over to the other side of the surgical center, where I would be having my MRI done. God blessed me with another delightfully smiling face there. The person explained to me how the MRI appointment would go. I felt the Holy Spirit, so I wasn't worried. I knew God was in control.

I was all prepared to begin when the nurse walked in and asked me to get on the table. From across the room, that hole in the MRI had looked a little bigger. I sat on the table, thinking, *Is that hole getting smaller, or is it just me?* I didn't have problems with small spaces before, but all of a sudden I did. I just tried to keep myself calm by breathing nice and slow. If you have never had an MRI before, let me tell you, there is beeping, shaking, pounding, and more sounds that you really don't want to hear after having a headache and other symptoms for several months.

When the MRI scan was over, the nurse walked back into the room with a look of serious disappointment on her face. She said, "I hope you feel better soon," and gave me a big, warm hug. I knew in my heart that it was my time for God to use me for his glory.

After my busy morning of running errands, Dr. Carlson called me on the phone. I heard compassion in his voice when he asked if I would call Joshua and if the two of us would meet with him as soon as possible at his office. I said, "Sure. No problem," with my perky, cheerful voice. I called Joshua and asked if he could meet me at Dr. Carlson's office. He asked if the doctor had said anything about my MRI. I said no. But I had already been blessed by God telling me in his own way. I knew what was going on and what was about to happen.

> Jesus looked at them and said, "With man this is impossible, but with God all things are possible."
> —Matthew 19:26 (NIV)

I arrived at Dr. Carlson's office first. Normally I would wait for Joshua before going into the doctor's appointment, but this time was different. I felt led to go inside by myself. We serve a loving God, one who wouldn't give me anything I couldn't handle. I walked to the front desk, where the friendly receptionist said, "Dr. Carlson is waiting. Come on back. I'll show you to the room." In the room, I waited for just a minute with butterflies in my tummy, wondering if I was right. Did I have a brain tumor? Those are scary words for most people to hear, but they weren't for me, as I was ready to take on the world with God by my side.

> Let not mercy and truth forsake thee: bind them about thy neck; write them upon the table of thine heart.
> —Proverbs 3:3

> Ask and it will be given to you; seek, and you will find; knock and the door will be opened to you. For everyone who asks receives; the one who seeks finds; and

> *to the one who knocks, the door will be opened.*
>
> —Matthew 7:7–9 (NIV)

Dr. Carlson walked into the room looking displeased and troubled. I could tell by the look on his face that he didn't want to tell me what the test results had revealed. I just smiled a really wide smile and then gave a giggle, trying to make him feel better about what he was about to say. I don't like to see him unhappy or upset. He took a big, deep breath and said, "Stephanie, I hate to be the one to tell you this, but what Dr. Buck and I saw from the couple of tests here in the office and now also in the MRI confirms what we were thinking. You have a very large mass on your left optic nerve. That's what is causing some of your symptoms." I just smiled and giggled a little more. I wasn't uncomfortable with, mortified about, or dissatisfied with what the doctor had just said.

He went on to tell me, "Stephanie, this is not something you can wait on. You'll need to get this taken care of right away."

There was a knock on the door, and in walked Dr. Buck. He was serious and to the point. "Stephanie, with a mass this size, you can't wait, so I went ahead and called your family doctor and asked him who he would recommend in Chicago to take a look at this large mass." Dr. Buck went on, telling me the plans for the next couple of days.

Then Dr. Carlson asked if I had any questions for him or Dr. Buck. I said no at first, but then I asked, "How big is this mass?"

Dr. Buck replied, "It's about the size of a baseball, maybe even a softball."

I felt the peace, love, faith, and mercy that God wanted me to feel during this time of receiving unfortunate news. I replied with a smile and said, "Okay."

Dr. Carlson wanted me to take one more test before I went home. He walked me to another room and explained how the test worked. Then he told me what I needed to do for this test. As the machine started, I heard Joshua's voice in the hallway. He was with the kind nurse, who was taking him to see Dr. Carlson and Dr. Buck in their room. I quickly started to pray. "God, I am strong. I can feel your Spirit, but I'm worried about Joshua. How's he going to take this news? He's brave, God, and a loving man, but when it comes to me being sick, he can't handle it. He hates it. He gets mad. Please, God, have mercy on him and let him feel the peace of the Holy Spirit that I feel because you picked me and not him. Amen."

> *But grow in the grace and knowledge of our Lord and Savior Jesus Christ.*
> —2 Peter 3:18 (NIV)

> *My brethren count, it all joy when ye fall into divers temptation; Knowing this, that the trying of your faith worketh patience. But let patience have her perfect work, that ye may be perfect and entire, wanting nothing. If any of you lack wisdom, let him ask of God, that giveth to all men liberally, and upbraideth not; and it shall be given him.*
>
> *—James 1:2-5*

Joshua was waiting in the private waiting room, hoping that Dr. Carlson would come in soon to ease his wonders. Finally, Dr. Buck entered. Joshua asked, "What's going on, Doctor?"

Dr. Buck said, "The MRI came back. It showed a mass on Stephanie's brain."

Joshua's jaw dropped. He began to tear up with disbelief. Then he asked, "How big is it?"

Dr. Buck said, "It's big."

Josh asked, "The size of a golf ball?"

Dr. Buck replied, "No. It's at least baseball size."

Josh said, "Oh my, that's big." Then Dr. Buck began to tell Josh about the next steps that needed to be taken. The doctor let my husband know he had already talked to the family doctor and received a recommendation for a doctor in Chicago. He also let

Josh know he made an appointment with that doctor for the next afternoon.

When I saw Josh for the first time after hearing the news about my mass, he started crying as I walked into the room. He looked very confused. I had come into the room calm, happy, under control, and smiling at him. We gave each other a big hug. The doctors finished up talking to both of us and asked us to keep them posted after our doctor visit the next day in Chicago. My husband and I walked out while holding hands.

When we got out to the parking lot, Joshua was in disbelief. He asked, "Why you, Stephanie? Why not me?"

I told him, "Just relax! It's going to be okay. We'll get things set up for the girls tomorrow and go see what the doctor has to say." I tried to calm him down and give him reassurance that we were going to get through this with God's help.

Josh made arrangements with his family so we could talk more privately to his parents about what we were told by the doctors. It was important for Josh and me to have an opportunity with his parents to come up with a plan for the girls. We both wanted the least amount of disruption to their routine, especially with school starting up so soon.

Josh and I jumped into our trucks and headed toward his parents' house, twenty minutes away. We had both taken our cell phones so we could talk to each other on the way down there. Josh was very quiet as I tried to make him feel better about the path God had chosen. It was simple for me to feel comforted in this new journey because God had given me the tools I needed to feel the joy and love of the Holy Spirit. Now I needed to guide Josh and to let him know that God's plan was great. I also needed to remind him that God doesn't make mistakes.

While Josh and I were talking, his brother Matt called to see if everything was okay, so Josh put me on hold. Apparently they had talked before Josh arrived at the doctor's office. Matt was concerned about what the doctor had to say. Josh asked his brother if we could meet him somewhere so we could talk to him in person. Matt suggested the parking lot of Kelsey's Steakhouse. So we headed over to Kelsey's. The details are a little fuzzy, but I remember that Matt said it was a shame that Josh and I had to go through something like this. He also told us to let him know if we needed anything.

Josh wanted answers to the questions he had right then: "Why, God, did you pick Stephanie and not me?" and "Why would you do this to a young mother with three little girls?" Struggling with the choice God had made, Josh began to get angry and upset with God. He needed to regain his composure before we arrived at my mother-in-law and father-in-law's house to tell them the news.

When we arrived at Greg and Earlene's house, I had a brief moment by myself. I used that time to say a quick prayer to God, asking him to help and guide me with the right words of wisdom and also asking him to help everyone else by giving them faith and the understanding that it was going to be God's choice, not theirs, when deciding what should or shouldn't happen to me and my family. It was important for Josh, Greg, and Earlene to remain positive, not only for me, but also for Hunter, Jaelie, and Violett.

Chapter 5
Sharing the News

Hunter (ten years old at the time), Jaelie (seven at the time), and Violett (four at the time) shouldn't have to worry about their mommy being sick or something worse. I needed to ask God to give Josh and me strength and self-control so that we could protect our loved ones who weren't ready to hear the news or who may have been fearful about what the future would hold for them.

When Josh and I walked through the doorway, sadness was on Josh's face. I was giggling. I believe that Earlene immediately knew that we were about to tell her bad news. Josh and I asked if Greg and Earlene would sit down so we could talk. At first, Earlene was stubborn and didn't want to sit, but she came around.

Josh began to tell his parents about my health problems over the last few months: dizziness, weakness, blurred vision, horrible headaches. We wanted to give his parents a general idea of what had been going on in our lives and also reassure them that I had gone to all my doctors to get to the bottom of the problem. Greg and Earlene listened eagerly to what Josh was saying. Josh finally composed himself and told them about my visit with Dr. Carlson and Dr. Buck. That's when his emotions took over and he started to cry. Fear was in Earlene's mind. She insisted that Josh or I say what happened at Dr. Carlson's office.

Josh said that I had a large mass on my brain. The tears rolled down Earlene's face as she heard the devastating news. Greg remained calm with his strength in the Lord, knowing that God was in control. They both said many times they loved us.

Earlene had many questions. Josh and I explained that Dr. Buck and Dr. Carlson had already talked to our family doctor and that he had recommended a doctor in Chicago. We wanted to reassure Josh's parents by letting them know an appointment was made for the next day, seeing as my brain tumor was an urgent matter.

A few minutes later, the phone rang. It was my brother and sister-in-law, Eli and Kendra. Greg and Earlene invited them over so that Josh and I could tell them the news and also so Earlene could ask Kendra, a nurse, all her questions.

When Kendra came through the door, everyone else in the room cried. I just kept smiling with confidence and joy. Once Kendra looked at me, she knew not to cry but to be joyful with me. Kendra knows I don't like drama or negative attention. I looked Kendra in the eyes and told her the news. She was a trouper, remaining strong for me and honoring my wish for no drama, even though I knew she wanted to cry.

After picking up the girls from Eli and Kendra's house, Josh and I went to tell my parents. My mom was the only one home at first.

Josh and I decided that it would be okay to go ahead and tell my mom instead of waiting for my dad to get home. My mom was crushed. She had spent most of her life putting her four children first, so upon hearing the news that I had a brain tumor, she was heartbroken. When my dad got home, my mom told him the news. He was prideful. He's the kind of man who doesn't cry or show emotion in front of his children, but he gave me a big hug.

Josh showed my parents the CD of my MRI. They were both amazed by how big the mass looked on the screen. We all kept saying how wonderful it was that I was still here on earth.

As far as informing our other family members and our friends, Josh and I decided to leave it up to my mom and mother-in-law to tell those other people the news and to ask for their prayers.

Chapter 6

Feeling God's Direction

We've all seen doctors who are just not very nice. My family doctor recommended to me a neurosurgeon at Northwest Hospital. Let me tell you, he wasn't pleasant. The appointment was painful for Josh. That doctor looked Joshua in the eye and said, "Look at your wife. She'll never look like that again after surgery. She'll be unable to walk, talk, and eat by herself again. She'll pretty much just be a vegetable." Talk about a Debbie Downer! But, see, I was okay with that man's bad attitude, because I did not feel God guiding me to this doctor or giving me reassurance that he was the one for my family and me.

The neurosurgeon's nurse, on the other hand, was a real trouper. Right before Josh and I left the doctor's office, we asked if he would give us some other doctors' names in the area to help us find another brain surgeon. The doctor replied, "Sorry, but no." Grr! He needed him some Jesus! As Josh and I were walking out, however, the nurse handed Josh a list of some doctors' names, saying that we may be interested in calling them. Praise me some Jesus! To that nurse, thank you for having a heart for helping others in need!

Once Josh and I got back to the car, his head was spinning with thoughts and emotions. Still, he started calling and making appointments with the three doctors whose names my trouper had given him. Pretty much every doctor whom Josh called was great about getting me in within five to seven days, but that wasn't quick enough. Josh wanted now care, not later care. This was when I needed to step in and give Joshua a talking to, because this was about God's plan, not Josh's plan.

A few hours later, the phone rang. The call was from two of our friends from church, Gary and Barb. They had magnificent news: they had talked to Barb's oncologist at Rush University Medical Center. Barb's doctor was able to get me in with Dr. Richard Byrne. What a perfect God we have!

That morning, I was full of excitement about meeting Dr. Richard Byrne and another doctor from another hospital. God gave me a mindful, worry-free attitude. He told me to wait until I felt the warm and fuzzy feeling inside before I decided which doctor was best.

My first appointment was with Dr. Byrne. His office was very clean, with a sensational check-in procedure and great nurses. I felt very welcome there once the first nurse came and took Josh and me back to the room. Then the fabulous nurse practitioner, Robin, came in and asked for the CD of my MRI. After this, she asked many questions about my health and then took my vitals. (Just so you know, Robin brings me much joy when I see her.) After going over some things, Robin said she was going to step out and talk to Dr. Byrne for a minute to update him on my story.

When Dr. Richard Byrne and Robin walked in, I felt safe but very giggly. I just kept smiling and giggling as the doctor talked to Josh and me. Dr. Byrne reassured Josh that there was hope and great discovery regarding this horrible disappointment. Both Dr. Byrne and Robin answered all of Josh's and my questions so that we both understood their assessments and instructions. They talked about the plans for before and after surgery, and then they said that I would require recovery time after I had surgery and once I returned home from the hospital.

Before leaving the office, I asked Dr. Byrne and Robin if I needed to cut my hair before surgery. With a simple grin on his face, the doctor replied, "If you don't cut your hair, I will, and I don't think it will be as nice as your hair stylist would do it for you, Stephanie." But I could tell he was tickled by the idea of cutting my hair.

Josh said that we needed to pray about the matter before we decided if Dr. Byrne was the doctor for me. We said our good-byes to the people at the office and then went on our way.

Stephanie N. Howard

As Josh and I were sitting in our car in the parking lot of the hospital, we talked about what had just happened. We needed to make a decision about going to the other doctor appointment, which was down the street. After Josh asked me a question about how Dr. Byrne made me feel, we both decided to cancel the other doctor appointment and to stick with Dr. Byrne and Robin. But just to be sure, we prayed first. We still felt the warm, fuzzy feeling after we prayed.

Chapter 7

Cut, Cut, Cut!

I had been growing my hair out for three years, trying to get it long. It was finally down to the middle of my back. That being said, I called my great Christian friend Rita to see if she would cut my hair within the next couple of weeks. She told me to come right over. As Joshua and I had about forty-five minutes to drive before we would arrive at her house, I started talking to him about how I could cut off all my hair in a fun way that I would always remember. A couple of ideas included buzzing it all off at once, like in the movie *G.I. Jane* with Demi Moore, or, more exciting, cutting twelve inches off the ponytail. Many of us have seen the results of a dramatic haircut during some of the makeover stories on TV: the drama, the tears, and the happiness that overwhelms everyone—the host of the show, and the family members and close friends of the party in question.

Joshua and I arrived at Rita's place shortly after talking. She welcomed both of us with open arms and tears in her eyes. I smiled at her and told her,

"Everything is going to be okay. We have God on our side, and a great, warm, and fuzzy doctor that God helped us find. I'm not worried a bit about what God's plan is for me. But Joshua, on the other hand, still needs a lot of prayer, comfort, reassurance, and joy. He needs to know that it's all in the Lord's hands."

More tears came down Rita's face. I gave her another big hug and said, "We need to have some fun cutting off all my hair, not cry over something I'm not troubled by." Joshua shook his head, probably thinking that his wife was crazy. Rita asked me to take a seat in her chair so we could get started. She had a hard time at first, knowing the reason for my cutting off all my hair. She asked me how I wanted to cut it. I said, "Joshua and I talked on the way over here and decided if you could put my hair in a ponytail, he would cut that part off. And you can finish with your magic." I giggled after saying that.

Rita smiled and said, "I think that's a great idea."

With my hair now in the ponytail, Rita explained to Joshua how to hold the hair in one hand and cut it with the other, holding the hair tight so the scissors could cut all the way through the ponytail. In the chair, I was laughing hard about Joshua taking this so seriously. The funny thing was that Rita still had to take off about four to six inches in order for my hair to be short enough for surgery. Joshua, Rita, and I all went to a place of delight for a minute, laughing when thinking of how many husbands had cut their wives' hair at such a life-changing time. But what I needed from my family and friends was simply their faith that, with God on my side, I could do anything he put before me. They could do the same if they just believed what the Bible says to us every time we pick it up.

Chapter 8

If You Ask, He Will Call Upon You

One Sunday, my brother-in-law Matt was teaching to the Young Adult Class this week's lesson from LifeWay literature. Matt asked the class if anyone had ever prayed for God to use them and their lives for whatever God's plan was for them. He went on to give an example of what that meant. As Christians, we often don't ask God during our Christian walk, "What are your plans for me, God?" Many times, we don't wait for God's guidance, or else we try to search for our path ourselves. Micah 6:8 reads, "He hath shewed thee, O man, what is good; and what doth the Lord require of thee, but to do justly, and to love mercy, and to walk humbly with thy God."

That Sunday school lesson stuck with me. I kept thinking, *Am I doing what God wants for me, or am I doing what I want? And am I helping God win souls?* During my prayer time with God that week, I asked him to use me whenever or wherever he thought I could be used to best glorify his name.

For a while, I thought that God didn't think I was ready to do what I wanted to do. I thought that God wasn't giving me the opportunity to glorify his name or win souls. But little did I know that God, the entire time, was preparing me for the miracle that I was about to partake in.

God shows us every day his love for his children. He gives us tools to handle challenges, trials, and temptation. Only Satan gives us the tools for a bad attitude and bad behavior. John 10:10 reads, "The thief comes only to steal and kill and destroy; I [Jesus] have come that they may have life, and have it to the full" (NIV).

There was a lesson in my LifeWay young-adult Sunday-school book that talked about that very same subject. And here are some points that helped me:

- I can choose to have a joyful attitude despite circumstances.
- I can trust God's loving heart always and forever.
- I can surrender to God's sovereign plan even when I don't understand it completely.
- I am sometimes tempted to show my anger. Talking without praying or first thinking about what I will say leads me down a wrong path. I am mindless of speaking out of anger until it's too late.

The Sunday before my surgery, our church family did a laying on of hands, which I'd never been a part of before. It was a stunning moment. The love I felt was remarkable. My sisters in Christ also prepared a time for fellowship and refreshments, which gave people the opportunity to offer me their thoughts and prayers. The group also presented me with gorgeous pajamas to wear during my stay in the hospital.

The night before surgery, I stayed up until 3:00 a.m. listening to my Christian music favorites and looking at pictures. Hearing the music and seeing the beautiful memories of my family that I had captured over the years made me cry for the first time since I had been diagnosed with a brain tumor. I wasn't crying because I was scared or fearful; rather, I cried because I knew I was going to miss Josh and the girls. Dr. Byrne hadn't been able to specify the amount of time I would be away from home for recovery.

On the day of my surgery, August 26, 2010, I was supposed to go into the operating room at 5:30 a.m. I wasn't worried a bit about what the Lord had planned for me and my family. Although my surgery was the first appointment of the morning, I had to wait to enter the operating groom. Unfortunately, there had been a very bad accident. It was important for the doctors and nurses to get the victim into surgery immediately. This person, whoever he or she was, was one of God's creations and needed help immediately—and I was happy. I could help in a small way by having patience.

It was good news for me because it gave me more time with family who wanted to come in and wish me well. Everyone tried their best to put on a happy face. I could see in their eyes the hurt they felt for not being able to take away my brain tumor themselves. I could also see their wondering, *Is this the last time I'm going to see Stephanie? Will she be the same happy-go-lucky girl we know and love so much?* But I knew the most powerful being was on my side: God!

After waiting a couple of hours and having fellowship with my family, it was my turn for surgery. I told Josh I loved him, asked him not to worry, and advised him to go get something to eat and then to relax. And, of course, I gave my Joshie a big kiss and a hug before I went rolling away.

On one of the fabulous days before my surgery, I had gotten to spend some time with my sister-in-law Kendra. During that time, I asked her if she would do me a great big favor. I asked her if she would have everyone who came to visit on the day of surgery sign my composition notebook to help me remember everyone who came to give their support and love. Kendra said she would be happy to help.

Let me tell you a few things about my sweet Kendra. She is a nurse; she's around the same age as I am; and she has a huge heart for helping people. Sometimes it's hard for me to ask her for help because everyone and their brother would call her when they want answers to all their health questions. She knows I don't like to be sad or to have sad people around me. She is one of my best friends and is like a sister to me. She tells me the way it is, and she pays attention to details. Kendra also encourages me to dream big and to accomplish the goals I set for myself.

As Kendra put it, my cheerleaders and prayer warriors were God, Pastor Ken, Pastor Bob, Mama Suzie, Papa Bill, my big sister Megan, my big brother Getty, my big brother Douglas, Maw Howard, Paw Howard, my big brother Matt, Matt's wife at the time, Jackie, my big brother Eli, Eli's sweet wife, Kendra, Gary, Gary's lovely wife, Barb, my same-day birthday buddy Barb H., Gerald, Denny, always-smell-good Meredith, Carrie, Carrie's daughter, Chelsi, Donna C., and Sharon M. In addition to this, Linda R. and Emily H. sent great cards. If I missed noting anyone, I'm sorry. I would also like to mention that a lot of different churches, family members, and friends prayed and were my cheerleaders for a good outcome.

I had packed some goodies and drinks the day before my surgery so that if anyone got hungry or bored they would have some food to eat—crackers, granola bars, gum, and healthy finger foods. Most of my family is Baptist; we can always eat. But my mother-in-law, Earlene, and Papa Bill packed junk food like chips, Suzy Q's, Twinkies, and chocolate-covered strawberries (what's waiting without chocolate-covered strawberries?). Silly people! But I love them.

Here's a little secret about all the people you see, whether it's your neighbor, your spouse, your coworker, or the person sitting next to you right now. Given that no one's life is perfect, we all need hope and healing. We can share with others the hope and healing that we've found in Christ. We need to remind ourselves and others that we need to wait and see what God has in store for our future.

When we step out of our comfort zones and step into our faith to serve others, just like Peter and John did in Acts 3:1–10, we start seeing amazing prayers and goals develop. These allow our hearts to be open to God's glory.

The day I had surgery, twenty-seven families and friends witnessed a miracle happen just like Peter and John did in Acts 3:1–10. All my loved ones joined in prayer for God's miracle to take place. And it wasn't just the people at the hospital that day praying for God's help. It was all different groups of families and friends, some of whom I knew and some of whom I didn't know, who heard my story through all kinds of ways—Facebook, e-mail, different churches' prayer request lists, and talking in the grocery stores. I was popular in the prayer department with God that day and in the couple of weeks leading up to my surgery. Everyone had my family's best interests at heart.

The day of surgery wasn't the end for me. Instead, it was the beginning, as seeds were planted for God to harvest. God touched not only my family and friends who were there that day, but also all of the people who heard about God's grace! It filled their minds with wonder and amazement, and with ideas of what else God could do, not only for me, but also for them and their loved ones. It changes people when they have their prayers answered. That's one of the reasons I wrote this book, to help people believe in God's love for us.

Chapter 9

Wait and See

My surgery took thirteen-plus hours. The doctors and nurses had their work cut out for them with my case. Josh was told after the surgery that I had my ups and downs during the operation and that it was pretty ugly inside my brain. But with persistence from everyone, including me, I would make it, they said. God had mercy on my family, my friends, and me on August 26. He believed that my work here on earth was not done.

Dr. Byrne was on his way to go to talk to Josh, Earlene, and my mom. He ordered some tests for me to see how my body would respond to being in surgery all day and being kept alive with assistance from machines.

Dr. Byrne had told Josh in a previous conversation that he would not be seeing him unless there was a problem, so when Josh was paged to a small waiting room away from everyone, he started to worry and to shake inside. Josh started to pray, saying, "God, whatever it is, just let Stephanie be okay so that our girls have a mother." Josh later said to me that it was hard at times during that day for him to breathe, to walk, to stay strong in hope and faith, and to know that everything was going to be okay. It was especially difficult for him at that moment, waiting for the doctor to arrive.

Dr. Byrne shook Joshua's hand and asked him to sit down so he could begin. He looked at Josh and said, "Josh, I know I said I wasn't going to come out here and see you unless there was a problem, but I wanted to tell you in person that all I kept thinking about when Stephanie was having challenging times during the surgery was, *Stephanie has three beautiful baby girls who need their mother to see them grow up and help them on their wedding day.*" (Dr. Byrne's is very sweet and has such a big heart.)

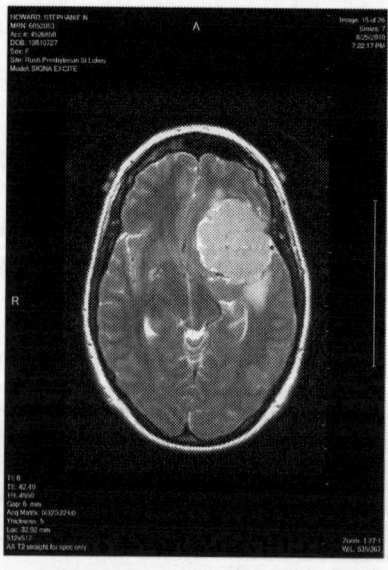

Then the doctor looked at everyone and said, "I believe we've got it all. Stephanie's okay. We won't know anything for sure until later, when we do an MRI and other tests. For the next couple of hours, we'll be keeping a close eye on her to make sure that she is comfortable. Stephanie needs to get rest. She's been through a lot today. In a couple of hours, family and friends can go see her." Josh, Earlene, and Mom could finally relax. They were all delighted to hear the glorious news; they started to cry for joy. They joined the pray warriors in the large waiting area. Everyone started to praise God for the wonderful miracle of answering their prayers.

In the ICU room late that night, family and friends waited to start trickling in, one or two at a time, to see for themselves what I looked like and how I was feeling. As I realized who they were, I tried to say hi, not knowing what they were seeing or talking about as they whispered (they were trying not to wake me). The medicine was starting to wear off, and my body felt heavy and shaky. I was getting sick to my stomach and wanted to throw up, but my head was hard to pick up off the pillow. The nurse who was working on the ICU floor was kind to help me feel more comfortable. She told me how to move my head so it would be easy if I did need to throw up. She said, "It's very common to feel that way after the day you had."

When Josh came in the room, I had just finished getting sick and was still shaking like a leaf. He said to me, "I can't believe how good you look after such a long day."

I looked back at him and said, "Did you like your chicken salad with the grapes?"

He smiled and then said, "Yes."

With all the family and friends amazed by God's miracle for that day, it was time for them to head home or to the hotel for a good night's rest. Little did they know what tomorrow would have in store for them.

Josh and Earlene stayed behind to keep me company and to be there in case I decided I needed someone to talk to or maybe to get me something that I wouldn't ask a nurse for. Unfortunately, Joshua got light-headed while visiting me at my bed. He needed to lie down for a couple of hours in a separate room. Some family and friends had told both of us that this day would be harder on Josh than on me. And they were right.

As I was trying to feel less sick to my stomach, I looked over at Earlene and asked if she would grab my iPod so I could listen to Christian music to help me concentrate on something else. After a few minutes of listening, I found that for some reason, even though the volume was turned most of the way down, the music seemed very loud in my ears. So I decided to place the earbuds next to me and listen.

The next morning, I woke up talking a mile a minute. I wanted to get out of bed as soon as I could, but little did I know I needed to stay in the bed because I had a catheter in my head and another in my bladder. It wasn't until later that the nurse informed me about my limitation. It was necessary for me to wait until Dr. Byrne or one of his associates came in to see the rapid progress I had made over the last couple of hours. I think I took everyone by surprise. I felt outstanding, and I wanted everyone I came into contact with to feel outstanding themselves.

Most people had in their heads that I was going to be a vegetable, unable to talk or move. But such wasn't the case. That's the fabulous thing about God: all things are possible. There is a beautiful song I love by Brandon Heath called "Wait and See." Some of the song's lyrics are, "He's not finished with me yet." God has big plans for me and for you. God wants you to tell your story.

As the hours went by, I noticed more and more that things were different: smells, tastes, sounds, sights. First, I could smell the apple juice across the room. When my brother Doug brought it to me and I drank some, it tasted sweeter than I remember apple juice ever tasting. Then my dad and Doug were talking to me and to each other. It was so loud, it sounded like they were yelling. And the nurse came in because she needed me to sign pages that hurt my eyes. Afterwards, I tried to read magazines that had bigger print, but that hurt too. As my dad and Doug sat in the room with me, I started feeling their shock, confusion, and worry inside my stomach. I couldn't explain what was happening, but I knew I was going to ask the doctor about it when he came in.

It was about 8:30 a.m. when the doctor arrived. He greeted me with a big smile and got straight to the point. He said he was very pleased with the progress I'd made during the short amount of time I'd been in the ICU. He asked if I had any questions for him. My first question was, "Why are my five senses so enhanced?"

He replied, "We rerouted your brain. Sometimes when you do that, it enhances the senses."

My second question was, "When can I get out of this bed and go to the bathroom on my own?"

He replied, "As soon as I talk to the nurses to take out the catheter."

And my third question was, "When can I go home?" Josh, the doctor, and some students all laughed a little.

The doctor replied, "One day at a time, Stephanie." I was okay with that. I just kept thinking about the time when I would be allowed to get up and go to the bathroom on my own. As the doctor was about to leave the room, he said, "Maybe if you have good reports from your nurses and the tests, we can get you into a regular room by the end of the day."

Shortly after the doctor left, the nurse came back, ready to remove the catheter. Hooray! Free of that, I was now faced with walking for the first time since my operation. The nurse asked me to take it slow, saying that going through a long surgery like mine can wipe a person out really fast. I am on Jesus's team, though, so all things are possible. The nurse told me several times to slow down, saying to me that it wasn't a race.

I made it to the bathroom, but I couldn't pee. How many times does that happen to you? You go to the doctor's office and they ask you to go into the bathroom and pee in a cup, and you freeze. Two minutes ago in your car, however, you could barely hold it. Funny! That's me every time.

As morning grew to afternoon and afternoon to evening, I became stronger and stronger. Before I knew it, the nurse said that she had reported in with Dr. Byrne. He said that because I was making such long strides in a successful recovery, it was time to move me to a regular room.

That evening, once I was settled into the regular room, my family and friends who were visiting started to see the determination God had for my quick recovery, his empowerment within me. They were a little taken aback by it. None of them had ever gone through brain surgery recovery before, so they hadn't known what to expect. That night after all the guests went home, I wasn't able to sleep very well. I wanted to talk, talk, and talk, but Josh didn't have any more energy. Once his head hit the pillow, he was out like a light.

I tried to sleep but wasn't very successful at it. You would think after a long day like mine with tests, an

MRI, and company that I would be tired, but I wasn't—not at all! So I just let my mind think about all the excitement that everyone shared with me about the last couple of days and how it affected them. It made me laugh. How zany my family can be when they're caught off guard! At about 1:30 in the morning, I finally closed my eyes for what I thought was hours, but it was only a few minutes. I catnapped like that most of the night until about 5:00 in the morning, when I tried to wake Josh. He wouldn't move. Finally, at 6:30, Dr. Byrne and his students came in to check on me and go over my reports from the day before and through the night. Also, he had to check to see if the tube was draining all the bad fluid out of my head.

Sometimes when remarkable gifts or blessings are right before your eyes, you find it hard to believe them with your heart. I believe that God wanted me to show all the people involved what he can and will do for his children.

God helped me realize that people weren't using all of their senses on that day, including the following:

- **Hearing** the Holy Spirit talking to them
- **Seeing** what beauty is front of them and the miracles that simply happen before them
- **Tasting** delicious food and drinks (and feeling joy and happiness after sensing the flavors)

- **Smelling** the delicious food that God provides us every time we sit down to eat, and the flowers that are part of his world
- **Touching** others by lending a hand, putting on a bandage, or even assisting someone across the street, showing compassion and a warmhearted spirit all the while

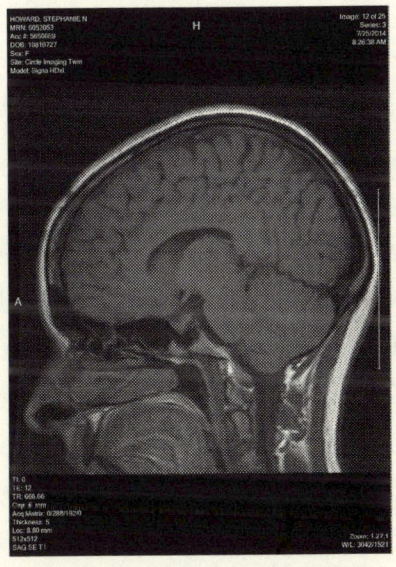

The joy that I wanted to share with all of God's doctors, nurses, workers, family, and friends he put in my path was incredibly important to me. It was on my third day in the hospital when I started singing all the songs that brought me happiness. And I would ask everyone who stepped into my room to join in. A lot of them at first were shy and nervous, but after I asked them a couple more times, they finally belted out a couple of verses from their favorite artists, such as Tenth Avenue North, Bob Marley, and even Michael Jackson. It made me smile a very big smile to see them having fun with me. When they sang, I smiled about the memory we were making by being silly, not about my recovery.

In the mornings, I called my dad, my brother Doug, and my sister-in-law Kendra, thinking they may be up and getting ready to start their morning. I wanted someone to keep me company. When one of them answered the phone, I started asking many questions just so they wouldn't hang up.

Every day when Dr. Byrne came to give me his report, I asked him if it was time for me to go home. He would shake his head in disbelief before kindly saying, "Let's have a couple more MRIs and blood tests, and time with your physical therapy, to make sure you're strong enough for your three girls and Josh." Dr. Byrne kept me in the hospital for four or five days. What a wonderful God we serve!

To be honest with you, I found it overwhelming at first to think about making plans for the girls' homework, schedule, practices, etc. I didn't want to forget that Dr. Byrne recommended that I have someone with me for the next two weeks.

Everything was happening very quickly, but I was delighted at the thought of being with my Hunter, Jaelie, and Violett. The thought of all of us under the same roof brought joy to my heart. When the girls and I first saw each other after my surgery, they all cried happy tears of joy, as they were pleased to finally be back with their mama. I smiled so much, my cheeks hurt.

After the excitement calmed down a little bit, the questions started. Jaelie was very worried, wanting to know if my hair was going to come back. Hunter wanted to make sure I didn't need anything. She wanted to make me a cozy bed on the couch and a cozy bed for her and the other two girls on the floor. Violett was young, so she wanted to know if we could have ice cream to make my boo-boo get better quickly.

At home, we were getting into a good routine—school, medicines, meals, etc.—for about four or five days when my health started to take a turn for the worse. The day was pretty normal, except that I was a little weaker than usual. Also, I wasn't hungry and I had a small fever. But I didn't think anything of it, because the doctors and nurses had told me that this would probably happen. Eventually my adrenaline would run out and I would start to relax, they had said. About 8:30 at night, I told Josh I was going to bed. I asked him not to forget to wake me at about 2:30 a.m. for my medicine. Josh said okay, but he mentioned that he wasn't ready for bed just yet. He wanted to watch ESPN, which was fine with me, because I knew Josh hadn't had a minute for himself for a few days. I believe it probably took five or ten minutes before he fell asleep.

At midnight, I awoke. I was shaking like a leaf, running a high fever, and becoming dizzy and nauseated, with discharge coming from my stitches and staples. Then, after fifteen to twenty minutes of sitting in my bed and wondering what was going on, I needed to try to walk the five to seven steps to the bathroom because I felt I was about ready to vomit. I had to pray a lot to make it to the bathroom successfully. I spent twenty or thirty minutes in the bathroom taking care of my problem while wondering what I should do: wake Josh or go back to bed and wait for him to get a little more sleep? What do you think I did? That's right, I went back to my room to wait and see what would happen in the next hour or two. That probably wasn't the best idea I had because everything increased for me—a painful headache, a fever as high as 103.5°, and the inability to walk to get Josh and ask for his help.

I tried to yell over and over, but my voice was no louder than a whisper. At that point, I knew I needed to pray and ask God to help me be strong enough to make it to the living room, about fifteen steps from my bedroom. Finally, after talking with God and asking him to stay with me as I walked to Josh to get his help, God gave me the strength. He stayed with me the whole time, telling me I could do this.

Once I made it to Josh, I scared him at first because he didn't know what was going on. But after a minute or two, he took a good look at me and knew that something wasn't right. He asked a lot of questions. I told him everything and showed him my pillow. He got on the phone to call his parents and Kendra. He asked his mom to watch the girls and get them ready in the morning for school, and then he asked his dad to drive us to Chicago because he was too nervous with everything that was going on to drive us himself. He called Kendra because she's a nurse. If there were any problems, she could help. The nice thing about Josh's family is that when you call them at any time, they answer; it doesn't matter how late it is.

Chapter 10

My Second Time in the Hospital

Josh called Dr. Byrne to let him know what was going on with my high fever, weakness, etc. While all that was going on, I was trying my best to make it to the girls' rooms to give them a kiss good-bye. I didn't know what was wrong with me or how long I was going to be gone. I wanted to make sure that I had my opportunity to love on my baby girls, because being away from them makes me feel uneasy. At those times, I feel like a bird looking for her baby birdie.

Once Greg, Earlene, and Kendra arrived, Josh explained the girls' morning routine to Earlene and then let Greg know he was driving. Kendra was to sit in the backseat with me.

On our way up to Rush University, I could feel the anxiety and tension from everyone in the car. Greg was trying very hard to keep Josh calm. I could tell that Josh was questioning himself about what went wrong. Kendra mostly kept quiet while she feathered my hair back and occasionally asked me if I was doing okay or if she could do anything for me. I answered that I was okay. I tried my best to concentrate on my breathing, remaining calm while using my fingers to circle the rim of a plastic bowl. I felt that if I did those things, I would be less likely to throw up again.

The ride up to Rush was a little shaky and bumpy. Greg was trying his best to get to the hospital in a timely manner. He pulled into the emergency room entrance. Josh went to retrieve a wheelchair so I could be rolled inside. The staffs were already aware that I was coming. After we entered the hospital, I went right back into the ER. I was first class, or VIP, at the moment. We all appreciated the special treatment, as we had no idea of what could be wrong. An ER doctor came into my room and asked several questions, which I answered to the best of my ability. He ordered blood work and urine samples. Other health-care workers checked my blood pressure and my temperature, the latter of which was very close to 104°. There was a pretty sure assumption that I was not going to be going home anytime soon. After I was in the ER for about two hours and had talked to Dr. Byrne, the staff there let me know that I would be staying overnight for observation and more testing.

The day was kind of restless for me, with lots of blood work, MRIs, CT scans, and checking of my vitals. Around 6:00 p.m., Dr. Byrne came in to let me know the results. He notified Josh and me that I had a very rare infection from the surgery and that I would be staying in the hospital for several days. I needed to take a course of strong antibiotics and steroids to help with the infection. After that, I would go in for a second surgery. This brought great sadness to Josh and me, as we realized that I would be away from the girls yet again for several days.

I felt it was necessary to start planning and scheduling right away. Josh assured me that everything was going to be okay. He said that he would accommodate the situation to the best of his ability. What a guy, right?

The second and third day were filled with my being pretty obnoxious by asking family, friends, and nurses every five minutes what time it was, if it was time for my medication or my walk, or if they would sing me a song. I was acting strange, but I was having a good time—and that's all that mattered at that moment. At first, everyone laughed and giggled and played along, but by the end of my stay people were pretty annoyed and asked me to please just be quiet and settle down. I was behaving this way morning, noon, and night. There was no downtime for me or for whomever was staying with me at the time. What did you expect? I was on a very high dose of steroids.

My surgery was on the fourth day of my stay in the hospital. Dr. Byrne explained to me and others that it would be quick. It was necessary to power-wash my brain to help the infection heal properly and effectively.

My family and friends who were there that day were a little unhinged by the idea that I had to have a second surgery, but they were relieved to know that the infection would soon be better.

Before the nurse came into my room to get me, my friends and family gathered together for a quick word of prayer and praise for all the joy and mercy that God had bestowed upon me and my family during this time of trial. Josh held my hand, gave me a couple of kisses, and told me he loved me. I, on the other hand, told him to have some fun without me so he could tell me all about it when I got back.

As I was being wheeled down to surgery, a miraculous thing was about to happen. Later that evening, my mom confessed her love for our Lord and Savior and was saved. Pastor Gamble helped lead her to the Lord. The Lord was filling my hospital room with hope, joy, and possibility.

Many times, people have asked me why I felt I was chosen to have a brain tumor. I have responded, "Hopefully to do the Lord's work and to guide others to what is possible with his hand and guidance leading them down the right path." That being said, if that is what is necessary to win souls and open the eyes of those around me, I would do it as many times as necessary. Sharing the wonderful gift that the Lord has for us is the best gift of all.

My surgery was very effective. I felt fabulous, other than that my back and tailbone were hurting pretty badly. I awoke in recovery with a Southern accent, which was rather entertaining. It lasted for a few hours. I remember saying to the nurse in my Southern accent, "Why do you make me feel this way? I don't like this. I don't like the way my back feels." I giggle at it now, as it was very humorous. My head didn't hurt at all, but my back was in extreme pain. I was blaming the nurse for bending me up like a pretzel during surgery.

She just kept saying, "Mm, honey, mm, honey, I know."

Once I was released from recovery, I was able to go back into my room. There I was greeted with smiling, happy faces of joy. At first, I believed it was because I was out of surgery; later, though, people told me it was because of my mother submitting herself to the Lord, which brought great joy to my heart and soul.

After my surgery, and thanks to the medicine, I got better and better every day. The doctors and nurses were very patient, for I was eager to get home as soon as possible to see my gorgeous little girls. But before I could leave the hospital, it was necessary for me to get physical therapy, have a good blood result, be educated on the PICC (peripherally inserted central catheter) line and how it works, get the tubing out of my head, know how to care for the thirty-five staples in my head, and be able to use the restroom independently.

A day or two before Dr. Byrne said I would be able to go home, Josh made calls to family, friends, and church members to make them aware of what I would need before I could go home. Mainly we needed someone to stay with me while Josh and the girls were away at school, at work, or running errands.

Family, friends, and church members were terrific, giving above and beyond what Josh and I needed. Just a few things they took care of during my second stay in the hospital were praying day in and day out for my healthy recovery; cleaning my whole house; making enough meals to last for weeks; baking goodies; sending cards, flowers, and gifts; making my whole family blankets (which we still have today and get cozy with in the fall and winter); sleeping over to let Josh get some rest; and driving Violett to and from preschool.

> Dear God-Loving Brothers and Sisters,
> Josh and I would like to thank you one more time from the bottom of our hearts and souls for being there for us in a time of need. Thank you for being God-loving believers, for playing with our girls, and for crying, joking with, and inspiring us and others with what is possible for God's children.
> The amount of love and energy that was shown to our family during

that highly challenging time will never be forgotten. The memories that were made during that time are still talked about today. God was so wonderful to put you all in our path.

Josh and I hope to be able to return the favor one day for you all, too.

Your God-loving brother and sister,
Joshua and Stephanie Howard

I had a mental checklist as I prayed to the Lord day after day, asking him to give me the wisdom and strength that was necessary to show good results to the doctors. I was finally released from the hospital after the ninth day. I was very attentive to the instructions, including those about a home-care aide who would be at my house in the morning to help me with any of my needs, my PICC line, and some blood work; no showering; no walking long distances; no driving; no being alone for long periods of time; and no heavy lifting. All of these things were necessary in order for me to go home. I couldn't wait to be reunited with my beautiful family!

Once Josh and I received the release forms and signed some paperwork, off we went, with many nurses wishing us the best for my quick recovery.

Praise me some Jesus, I was going to have the opportunity to hold my baby girls as long as I wanted. For some, that might've been a very long time—nine days in the hospital—but for me, it went by very fast with the Lord by my side. He helped me feel like it was a blink of an eye, and he gave me the comfort and joy of knowing that my girls were in good hands during that time.

Chapter 11

Home Sweet Home

The adrenaline that was running through my body when I arrived home was so invigorating that it was scary for the girls. I didn't want to sit still; I wanted to talk a mile a minute and to hear all about what I'd missed from the girls' lives in the last couple of weeks of school, playtime, and friends. There was so much to catch up on. After I spent a few hours hugging, kissing, and questioning the girls, we were all content just to hold each other, watch movies, and giggle.

For about two and half weeks, people were coming and going, dropping off or picking up something or someone. Day after day it was like a giant party with all the family, friends, and home-care staff who wanted or needed to see me. I received many blessings during that time. It was unbelievable. The stories and songs I heard about God's mercy and love for my loved ones were remarkable, and the rejoicing that took place in my living room and kitchen has changed my home. My walls are filled with stories and songs of God's loving praises and joy. That's what makes a home beautiful—the stories and songs that are told and held in it for the family and their friends to see.

It was all fun and games at first, but as the days went on, I had just one day and night after another with little or no sleep. At this point, I had about twenty-one days of no more than four hours of sleep a night. No matter how I tried to close my eyes, I kept thinking about something I wanted to talk about right then. I couldn't watch TV because it hurt my eyes and ears, and I couldn't read a book because doing so made me dizzy.

The medicine dosage to prevent seizure and hemorrhaging was stopping me from being able to sleep or rest for a long period of time. I felt that the dosage was too high, but I understand that the doctor was being cautious.

I was very grateful for all the love and attention that I was receiving during those few weeks, but by the second or third week I wanted my independence back. I wanted to go to the bathroom and shower by myself with the door shut and without worrying about falling or doing something I wasn't supposed to. I wanted to cook and clean for my husband and girls by myself. I felt that it was time for everything to go back to normal.

Josh and some other family members were a little nervous about my being left alone, but Josh promised me he would e-mail Dr. Byrne about it. Dr. Byrne wrote in reply that we could talk about it when he saw me in a couple of days. That appointment couldn't arrive fast enough.

If your loved one is telling you how she is feeling or what she believes about the way she is feeling, then you should listen, because only God and your loved one know her body best. During the beginning time of recovery, I felt that no one was listening to me or cared about what I had to say about my wants or needs. I tell you the truth; it made me very angry inside, because I never lied to anyone when they asked me questions about my health. If ever I felt sick, dizzy, nauseated, overwhelmed, etc., I would tell a person right away. Please remember this when or if you have a loved one who is sick. Hear what the person is telling you about him- or herself.

While sitting in Dr. Byrne's office, waiting and praying for what he was going to say about my restrictions, I was hoping he was going to say, "Stephanie, you look great and we're stopping the medication. You can go back to your regular routine at home with Josh and the girls." Unfortunately, Dr. Byrne said that I would have restrictions for a few more weeks. Being independent, I was not happy about that, but I smiled and said okay, knowing I was going to pray a little harder for God to answer my prayers.

I did get my thirty-five staples and six or so stitches out that day. Violett was with me and Josh during that time, and she had her face right up in there, observing what the doctor was doing. Violett was fearless and funny, asking the nurse if she could take out some of my staples. The nurse told Violett she could take out the last one. Boy, did she, with help from the nurse, of course.

On our way home, I had it in my mind that I was going to pray until I got my way about the medication situation. I didn't like the ways the meds were making me feel—sleepless, annoyed, and angry. That's not the kind of person I am or want to be.

A couple of days later, I finally got my prayers answered! Before I could be taken off my medication, I needed to have a psychiatric evaluation and also visit Infection Control for my last checkup. After that, I would be home free. I continued and continued to pray for God to keep blessing me with answered prayers.

Our wonderful God blessed me once again with good reports from the psychologist and Infection Control. Infection Control said I needed to administer my medicines one more day, and then the home-care nurse could take out my PICC line in the morning.

> I thank my God upon every remembrance of you, always in every prayer of mine making request for you all with joy, for your fellowship in the gospel from the first day until now.
> —Philippians 1:3–5 (NKJV)

Chapter 12

Praying for Friendship

My brain surgery helped me overcome one of my fears: friendship. I'm talking about a friendship that is true and caring, the kind of friendship that you read about in books or see on the Hallmark Channel. I've had a lot friends come and go in my life, but I hadn't had a true friend until I prayed to God to show me the way to put myself out there for people to see the true Stephanie. I was afraid of being rejected and judged because of who I was. But God showed me that I didn't see, or believe, the one-of-a-kind person I am: I believe in God; I love to give gifts; I love to talk to people and listen to them tell me about their successes and problems so we can pray to or praise God; and I want to help out whenever needed.

Shortly after praying and talking to God about my need of a true friend, he reunited me with a friend from my past, Mama Karen. Mama Karen and I became true friends instantly. We have very much in common. We both believe in our Lord and Savior, have our families in church, and are involved in church ourselves. We both have all girls; she has four. We come from the same town and know all the silly stories about the people there. We both like to be funny at softball practices and games just to make the time pass a little more enjoyably. In fact, Josh coached two of Karen's girls, and that's how Karen and I reunited.

Our friendship had grown so much by 2012 that Karen and I decided to go on a girls' trip together, my first. We had a lot to celebrate. That August was the second anniversary of my surgery, and Karen was celebrating moving to Indianapolis and joining her girls with her soon-to-be husband, Scott, in June. Karen was going to be having brain surgery herself for a slow-growing brain cancer. We both believed that God allowed our paths to cross so we could help each other out.

The vacation gave us the opportunity to talk about how I was feeling since my surgeries and how Karen was feeling about her surgery coming up. There were no phones, bosses, husbands, fiancés, or kids to interrupt us. We knew the girls were in good hands with Josh. Yes, all seven girls stayed with Josh while we were gone, but Josh was good with a big team of girls. He had been coaching softball for many years at that point, so he knew how to handle getting the girls ready for breakfast, school, practices, dinner, and bedtime. He did an outstanding job. Karen and I didn't have to worry a bit during our time of fellowship with much sun and rest. Josh would send pictures of the girls with their seven cereal bowls and seven toothbrushes lined up in a row in the morning, with a cute little saying like, "I don't know what you moms are talking about; being a stay-at-home parent is easy." But after a day or two went by, Josh changed his tune.

Praise the Lord for Karen's and my friendship. During our trip, we shared some much-needed counseling and guidance to let each other know we weren't alone.

I hold Karen's and my relationship dear to my heart because she's a God-loving woman who sees me through my ups and downs. Karen understands me, and I don't have to worry about her judging me later for things I said or did. She is one of my truest friends. I thank the Lord for that.

God and Karen have helped me overcome my fear of true friendship. Developing my relationship with Karen was the beginning of my new outlook on people around me. God's and Karen's guidance and leadership led me down a different road, and today I am not afraid of true friendships coming in my direction. I welcome them with open arms.

> Be aware of acquaintances versus true friends in your life. When you simplify your friendships, you are well on your way to leading a richer, fuller more joy-filled life.
>
> —Bill Hybels

Chapter 13

Pride and Depression Don't Mix with God's Plan

Satan was gaining the victory about a year after my brain surgeries. He took me to a place of shame, embarrassment, and fear. I'd become a person who didn't want to go anywhere or do anything with anyone.

I was turning to my Bible, to Christian books and magazines, and even to my favorite Christian songs for guidance. You would think with the right material, I should have been able to turn the tide of depression. But without fully giving my heart to God, it was not possible.

I'd have the right mind after church or after reading my Bible, but it would last only a minute, until I'd walk out the church doors or stop reading my Bible. I'd feel the shame and embarrassment all over again. God was giving me the love and support I needed, but it soon disappeared from my heart and mind. Satan was winning the war.

I was guilty of criticizing all the people I loved, especially the one person who was my biggest fan, Josh. I wasn't happy, so I didn't want him to be happy either. The expression "Misery loves company" applied to me at that time. I started to realize I was beginning to push family and friends away to protect them from my anger and frustration.

I didn't want to bring my remorse and guilt to family members' and friends' attention. I felt I wasn't being the mother, wife, daughter, or friend I needed to be.

I had no patience, understanding, or reasoning with the girls or Josh. It was my way or the highway. The house had to be perfect at all times—beds made, clothes put away, and everything cleaned up.

My face said, "Look out! Mama's mad!" I was trying daily to find guidance all around me through songs, books, and the Bible. I wasn't hearing what God was telling me. I had too much pride in myself to ask God for help so I could get back on track. I thought I didn't need God to solve my problem of being unhappy or of being out of control when it came to my emotions.

But we all know that a person can't do anything without God's help. Satan had me thinking very little of myself, which showed me how powerful Satan can be. He made me think I didn't need God during the most important time of my life. Satan was ruining my relationship with God. I didn't want to get out of bed. I cried often, and I felt lost and empty on the inside.

There was article in *HomeLife* magazine called, "How You Can Tell if You're Depressed." I laughed to myself, because I saw this as God's way of saying, "Open your eyes, Stephanie. You need my help. You can't do this on your own." That's when it hit me: Satan was winning—I was depressed!

Months later, I finally talked to my doctor about my depression. I realized that I had made everything about me: *my* God, *my* family, *my* joy, *my* plan, *myself*.

I was struggling to get out of bed every day, wanting to keep the covers over my head and to hide from the world. I was crying morning, noon, and night. I was afraid that I'd disappoint God, Josh, and the girls. I had no control. I tried to put on a happy face and think positively for the day ahead, but I was filled with guilt and remorse because I couldn't change the way I felt about myself and others. I wanted out of this place of sadness, darkness, and isolation. I felt alone with no hope.

As the seasons changed, my darkness and uncertainty grew. I walked around thinking that everyone was wrong while I was judging them. And I saw myself dwelling on family and friends, for example, the way they looked and acted when they were with me. Family and friends would call to check on me and the girls. I would say to myself, "These people are asking me too many questions." I couldn't handle it. It was driving me crazy. I wanted to scream at the top of my lungs, "You're taking all my energy!" I couldn't focus. I was distracted very easily and had a quick temper with Josh and, sometimes, the girls. I saw them all as if they were judging me. I believed that not one person trusted me to handle my day-to-day life as a wife and mother. I wanted to regain control, my voice, and the trust of others.

The power of Satan is convincing; he loves to confuse. He was making my thoughts unwise and unreasonable. They were certainly not led by God. Satan wasn't allowing the Holy Spirit to guide me. The Holy Spirit was reminding me from time to time, saying, "Stephanie, you are wrong about Satan having the control over you! I am God. I am and always be will be your strength, love and guidance. I don't want you thinking and acting this way. I don't want you or anyone else to have thoughts like that. All the evil and judgment you are feeling is out of character. Stephanie, you need to think! Is this how you want others or, more importantly, God to see you? Why would you want to hurt God or the people you love this way?"

That reminder from God would soon wear off. Worldly views would break free in my mind, justifying my thoughts and actions. I got to a point that when the phone rang, I wouldn't answer it. The few times I did, I would keep the conversation short and sweet, not giving myself the opportunity to say something I would regret or dwell on once I hung up the phone. When it came to special occasions, I made excuses for why I wouldn't go. I was pushing away my loved ones and, most of all, God and the wonderful man he had sent me to spend eternity with.

Josh and I would be up night after night for hours after putting the girls to bed, trying to figure out a way to help me feel God's love. Some nights ended well, but most nights ended with my getting defensive and criticizing Josh, expressing how disgusted I was when he touched me. What pushed my buttons the worst was when Josh told me he thought I needed to go see a counselor or maybe get on medicines. I wanted to push him as far away as possible when he said those things. He was talking nonsense and was out of line by suggesting I take medicine. He knew how much I hated taking meds.

Satan was helping me. The love that Josh had for me during this time was remarkable and unexpected. Many men would walk away and not look back. I was handed over to the power of Satan. My judgment was clouded by him, and he was helping me change my path by removing the blessings that God had given me and my family. My family and friends would tell me, "Josh is one of a kind, a Prince Charming." But my behavior was ungodly. I was seeing my husband in a different light, as a target for my anger. I was awful to this prize that God had given me, this gift I was supposed to cherish and live happily ever after with. I'm not the type of person who thinks or wants the worst. I shouldn't say evil, hateful words that are unforgettable and that simultaneously lower Josh's self-esteem as a father and husband.

Prideful people don't realize their needs. And that's what I had become: prideful. I wanted to fix all my problems I had with my life and with Josh by myself. I thought my problem was all in my head. I didn't need help from God or anyone else. Wrong! I was seeking the wrong kind of independence, and I didn't recognize that as a sin. God always resists those who oppose his rule and choose not to follow him.

I needed to humble myself. I had too much pride and didn't want to believe that God had power over me. Avoiding and resolving conflicts without God's help is a merry-go-round of craziness. I wanted to cover my whole body with the armor of God to guard me from Satan's power.

Resolving my problem was going to take time and patience that I didn't have. I wanted it resolved with a snap of the fingers. My return to having patience and an understanding of God's Holy Spirit required me to believe that Christ was in control of me. God was trying to keep me from resisting his grace and forgiveness. Previously, he had used his help, favor, and blessing to humble me. But humble people don't demand their own way. Humble people admit their needs to God. Humble people don't seek the things of the world to validate themselves. Humble people find grace from God to start over and receive new strength. God will be there waiting with open arms.

Unfortunately, my behavior continued this way until August of 2012, two years after my surgeries. Josh and I were both hiding this bad trial in our marriage from family and friends, but we discovered what God's love really means and what a fantastic God we serve.

I wanted to give God glory, but I loved to take care of my trials myself. How many people feel that way? I think to myself that my problems are very small compared to those of everyone else in the world. I also think that I can take care of Stephanie. Here's the thing, reader: God wouldn't say over and over in the Bible that you're never alone if he didn't mean it.

God will provide a way to escape a problem and help us stand up amid any temptation we face. Break free of Satan's control. Give your heart and mind to God.

I was depressed. It was very hard for me to understand I, Stephanie, depressed. I love to make people smile and be happy. I love to help them forget their problems for just a minute. But all of a sudden I was afraid of people. I couldn't imagine someone thinking that I wasn't good enough, that I couldn't do something I put my mind to.

I needed encouragement, but not the kind I was ready for: talking to the doctor. I needed to stop downplaying the influence that my feelings and actions were having on my life. This was hurting me and not helping me grow in Christ.

I prayed to find the person with whom I would be the most comfortable when talking about the problems I'd been having. God led me to my obstetrician, who was reasonable, understanding, and easy to talk to. She knew me inside and out. She was my doctor for all three of my pregnancies with the girls. The ups and downs of caring for an expectant mother and delivering a child are complicated. Dr. Jones understood me. She never judged my silly questions, no matter how crazy they may have seemed. Dr. Jones and I made a good team in my times of need before, so why not now? Why not when I was lost and confused?

When I made the appointment with Dr. Jones, I thought I might not even have the strength to talk to her about the problems that I was having at home with Josh and the girls, and elsewhere with other people. As I was driving to my appointment, I talked to myself, trying to make up my mind: did or didn't I want to let Dr. Jones know how tough the ups and downs had been over the last eighteen months?

Chapter 14

Facing Reality

Jesus doesn't simply want us to trust in him or to find our hope in him for certain things. He wants us to find hope in him for all things. He wants us to trust him for everything. Trusting Jesus means allowing him to do for you what you cannot do yourself.

When I saw Dr. Jones, she asked me how I was feeling since I had my surgeries. That's when I started to shake like a leaf in the fall. I began telling Dr. Jones what she would want to hear from an outgoing, upbeat Stephanie.

Then, after a few minutes, I struggled to ask the questions that I had on my mind. I wasn't comfortable. I looked fearful. I put my faith in God that it was going to be okay, and I convinced myself that I was in a safe place, one where God wanted me to be in order to get the help that I needed. I said, "Dr. Jones, is it common for women my age to feel overwhelmed and stressed out to the point that they don't want to get out of bed, and if they decide to face the world that day, they end up just crying several times over the littlest problems? Is it also common to not want to be sexual with a great-looking man like Josh, who would do anything and everything to make someone happy?"

We both giggled at the same time. Dr. Jones smiled at me kindly and said, "Stephanie, I want you to know that what you're feeling is very normal. You have three beautiful girls, a wonderful husband, and a busy lifestyle." She went on to ask, "When was the last time you and Josh went on a date, just husband and wife without the kids? You know, it's very important for a married couple to make time for just each other without the kids so the couple can grow, even if it's just for an overnight or a long day together." I agreed as she went on, saying, "It's also very important for you to take some time for yourself to regroup and recharge. How can you be the wife and mother that you want to be if you don't take time? You need to find something that you like that doesn't require work. You need something that relaxes your mind and body."

As Dr. Jones was offering all these helpful suggestions, I was thinking to myself, *Clearly I'm not that good at making time for myself or going on dates with Josh.*

After I talked with Dr. Jones on two different visits, she and I came up with the idea that I needed to give medicine a try. Despite what my pride was telling me to do, my doctor assured me that things should get better after a couple of months of using some helpful tools such as praying, taking time for myself, talking to Josh about a plan for my recovery, taking one day at a time, not putting so much pressure on myself to please everyone, and learning how to say no. These things would give Josh and me a better understanding of what we were facing with the sadness and depression that I was experiencing on a daily basis.

Within a matter of weeks, the new medication had already started taking effect. I wasn't crying as often, and I noticed myself smiling and laughing a little more than I'd done in months. When I read my Bible, I could concentrate on what God was trying to tell me.

Chapter 15

God Makes Me Stronger

With God by my side, I've continued to get stronger and stronger mentally and physically, every day. God has opened my eyes to the wonderful road ahead. By reading the great resources listed below, I have drawn closer to the Lord:

- My Bible (as often as possible)
- Beth Moore's *Breaking Free: The Journey, the Stories*
- LifeWay Sunday school lessons from 2011, 2012, 2013, and most of 2014
- *HomeLife* magazine
- Joyce Meyer's *Beauty for Ashes*
- Karol Ladd's *The Power of a Positive Mom*
- Ken Sande's *Peacemaker*
- Bill Hybels's *Global Summit*
- Beth Moore's *Global Conference* and *Children of the Day*

> When my heart is overwhelmed: lead me to the rock that is higher than I.
> —Psalm 61:2

> I am with you and will keep you wherever you go.
> —Genesis 28:15 (ESV)

> But the Lord stood with me and strengthened me.
> —2 Timothy 4:17 (NASB)

Once I received the okay from Dr. Byrne in 2011, I started trying to become a runner. In the last few years, I've run or walked the Popcorn Panic 5K (with Josh in September 2011); the Turkey Trot 5K (three times: one time with Josh in 2012; another time with Joshie and Jaelie in 2013; and another time with Jill, Jill's lovely daughter, and Jaelie in 2014); the Big Ten Network 10K (with Josh in 2012); the Brain Tumor 5K (twice: once with my big brother Getty in 2013, and once with my friends Karen, Jill, and Morgan in 2014); the New Year's Resolution 5K (with Josh in 2012); the Women Rock 9.6 miles (with Jill, Kelli F., Kelly B., Tracey, Kate, Betsy, Candice, and Beckie in 2014); and the Hot Chocolate 15K (with Josh in 2014).

On the physical side, I need to say a verse to myself when I'm feeling weak and want to stop during my runs:

"I can do all things through Christ who strengthens me" (Philippians 4:13).

Praying and setting goals with God by one's side are the best tools I can recommend for anyone who is interested in trying something new. I can't tell you about one time in my walk with God that he hasn't encouraged me or directed me down the right path.

There have been countless times that I wanted to stop during one of my runs, but God kept pushing me and gave me the strength to finish.

In the spring of 2012, I had prayed to God that he would give me the strength and confidence that I needed to run my first 5K nonstop. As I started doubting myself right off the bat during my warm-up walk, I prayed more and turned on my praise music. I noticed that something was moving in the trees; at first, I thought it was a squirrel. I didn't think anything of it and just kept walking, but then as I walked a little more I saw the trees moving again, and this time the motion was a little higher up in the trees. So I stopped and looked harder into the trees that were shaking, but I still saw nothing there. Finally, I heard the Holy Spirit say to me, "Stephanie, I want you to look up." When I did, there it was—the brightest, biggest, most stunning rainbow I had ever seen. This was not a rainy day. In fact, it was gorgeous outside. I did run that first 5K nonstop after seeing the picturesque rainbow that day, and I made remarkable time, too. Praise the Lord for his strength and wisdom!

God has helped me to overcome my fear of making true friends, and with that I've found a great group of women who rejoice in my good fortunes, pray for me in times of need, and don't judge me when I fall and make mistakes. They're willing to pick me up and dust me off. We have an understanding that we are just learning and growing every day, not forgetting why God has allowed us to wake up every morning and go to sleep every night with blessings in our hearts.

God has inspired me to get involved in what is possible when I've allowed him to guide me and give me direction. In the last few years, God has been preparing me for my calling—to be an inspiration to my brothers and sisters in Christ and to plant the seeds for family and friends who aren't sure about God's full potential or possibilities.

What God and I have accomplished in this short season is remarkable. I'm proud of my ups and downs, and the things that I've overcome, because I wouldn't be the happy, outgoing, God-loving person I am today without all the trials and tribulations in my past.

Josh and I are still raising our girls in a God-loving home. We attend church, praying to and praising God for all our marvelous blessings. Josh is still growing in the Lord and working for the same God-fearing company that he has been with for the last twenty years. Now he is going back to college to further his education. He is still involved in leading and encouraging the young girls' softball teams so the girls can be the best they can be with the gifts and talent that God had given them.

Hunter is in eighth grade. She is trying to find her direction when it comes to the Lord's work. She is also seeking to discover her place and talents in the world. She is looking for true friends. In school, she seeks to be a leader, not a follower, in her activities, which include drama, softball, singing, and attending Wednesday night youth club.

Jaelie is in fifth grade. She is outgoing in her new Team Lead Group at school, the purpose of which is to encourage children in all grades to make good choices, to know the difference between right and wrong, and to be positive with the new challenges they face in school. Jaelie is also learning how to become a great second-base player and catcher for her softball team. She's trying to reduce the negative thoughts that echo in her head when she makes a mistake. Josh and I tell her all the time how great she is, but the battle is for her and God to wage.

Violett is in second grade. She's still thinking the world is her stage. She has no fears about making new friends or trying something new as long as her mommy is right next to her. She works hard on schoolwork, gymnastics, and pleasing her teachers and parents. She loves to entertain with fun jokes and stories about what happens around her, and she doesn't forget any details of a good story.

I just realized that I didn't mention anything about how Josh's and my relationship is doing. I would like to address that point right here.

It brings me great joy to share the news that, with all the ups and downs over the last few years in our life, Josh's and my marriage is still going strong and thriving. God and Josh never give up on me. "And say ye, 'Save us, O God of our salvation, and gather us together, and deliver us from the heathen, that we may give thanks to thy holy name, *and* glory in thy praise'" (Chronicles 16:35).

Thank you, God and Josh, for loving me and believing in me unconditionally. Thank you for allowing me the opportunity to bring glory to God's kingdom. I'm eternally grateful with all of my being.

Josh's and my relationship has grown from being a landscape of darkness to being a landscape of beauty. Don't get me wrong, we still get weeds in our landscape every now and then. But the God we serve is a loving God who wants to help us at any and all times.

My family all love to sit down at the dinner table and talk about our praises and the good fortunes that we receive each day. We've had the fabulous opportunity to do some traveling as a family over the years to places like Orlando, Florida; Boyne, Michigan; and Boston, Massachusetts. We've also gone to Cubs, Bears, Colts, and Blackhawks games. When at the sporting events our family can become a feisty Christian bunch, entertaining the fans around us with our heckling of each other. Good family fun!

I am on my road to recovering from my third brain surgery because of an infection, but you can hear about that in my next book. I'm thirty-three years old and full of life, love, and happiness. I love to talk to anyone I encounter along my path. I try to bring people joy in their day, no matter where I am—in a coffee shop, at a softball game, at the girls' schools, or in a grocery store. When I see a need that needs to be met, I put myself out there just as Jesus did for us in the Bible. I live almost every moment to the fullest. I'm still taking naps at any opportunity I get. I'm learning to become an inspirational speaker and a leader to make God famous. I'm also training for the Hot Cocoa 15K this November.

I want to move ahead each day and give my problems and worries to God. I seek to move with the positive, change the negative, keep learning, and have an open mind to what God has in store for me and my future.

Writing this book and speaking to others has been very challenging for me, although it is edifying to recall that many men and women of the Bible were tested likewise and were a testament of God's love and mercy. God has never failed me. Praise me some Jesus! Amen.